Lets start off with the basics: what is witchcraft?

If you were to look up witchcraft in the dictionary, you'd probably get some opinionated definition calling it "evil". Witch craft is not evil. Witchcraft is the use of "magic" of course, but its not evil. Its beautiful in nature, and best of all witchcraft helps you believe in the most powerful thing in the universe: you .

There are two religions that practice witchcraft: Wiccan and Pagan. Wicca is a more modern form of witchcraft, and they worship two gods and follow traditions of pre-Christian religions. On the other hand, Pagans follow Christian beliefs and worship several gods or nature itself and may or may not practice witchcraft. it's all about your preferences. you don't even need to associate with any of these religions to practice witchcraft as well. Witchcraft is more individualized to yourself. You could do them as a Christian (Christians already use witchcraft without acknowledging it).

Onto the good stuff: Tips and tricks for practice

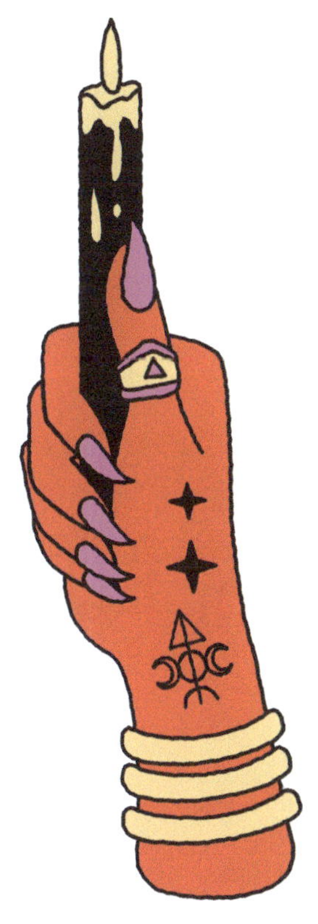

1.   **Candle colors are unique to the spell you're doing.**

**In order to help with your intentions, you may use a specific candle while doing a spell for those intentions. These candles dont even have to be fancy,
they can even be Birthday candles.**

White- Purity, peace, the goddess, and can substitute any candle color
Black- Banishing, Protection, rejects negativity
Red- Strength, fast action, and fire element
Green- money, personal growth, earth, and healing
Purple- spiritual power and psychic abilities
Brown- house, animals. and special favors
Orange- General success, property deals, Legal matters, and Justice
Yellow- air element, the sun, intelligence, memory
Blue- communication, travel, inspiration, and calm
silver- intuition, dreams, the moon, and feminine energy
gold- wealth, masculine energy, luck, power, and hapiness

2. You don't need to spend a lot of money to get started in your craft

It helps to get some materials to get started, sure. Don't over do it. Materials from the dollar store can do just fine. Witchcraft is mostly about intention. Intention is everything. If you believe in yourself, you can manifest to your hearts content.

3.Manifestation

Some people consider manifesting as a form of witchcraft, simply because things happen for you just like magic. There are many ways to manifest. You can:

1.   Journal your intentions and desires
2.   Make a manifestation picture board
3.   repeat positive affirmations to yourself, starting with "I Am." because you are your manifestation.

The most important thing you need to do while manifesting is
Keeping a positive mindset.
You must be positive in order to receive what you desire, or else you'll be stuck where you are.

4. Deity work

if you're brand new, I do not recommend working with any deity. If you're not careful enough, it can be a trickster or some sort of negative spirit trying to attach itself to you.
I would wait for the proper signs and do plenty of research on the deity you wish to work with before doing so.

5. connect with nature

One of the best ways to get in tune with yourself and the energies around you is to go outside.
You can meditate in nature, go on a nature walk, or even hug a tree.
A big part of witchcraft is being one with nature, and taking some of those small steps will help your craft.

6. Always cast a protection circle for spell work

Protection is very important while practicing your craft. You don't want to be swayed by evil entities , so always make sure to cast a circle of protection.
There are multiple ways to cast a protection circle, from making a salt circle, a protection candle, a smoke cleanse, etc.
My favorite, and very simple, way of protecting myself before spell casting is cleaning my space with an incense, while saying:

" Only entities of love and life are invited. All others are not invited. Leave now."

7.practice grounding

Grounding is a way to root yourself into reality, be one with the Earth, and a way to keep a level head. Meditation and deep breathing are great ways to ground yourself, as well as healing your root chakra. Healing your root chakra is pretty easy. As you meditate, inhale good and light, towards the tale end of your spine, exhale all the bad energy. I find that this helps me the best, but there are crystals, such as black tourmaline, that can help you out too.

8.music can be used for spell work

Making your own catchy tunes, or using others people have made, is a great way to help manifest and/or cast spells. At certain frequencies, manifesting or spell work becomes easier. Our bodies are like sponges, we absorb frequencies from music, water, and anything else that carries those frequencies. Chanting is also a good way to do spell work too, so it can be embedded in your head, and you may even repeat it to yourself later on. A catchy Rythm can do alot!

9.Crystals can enhance your craft

Different crystals have different purposes in your craft. For example, pyrite is good for money manifestation. You can place crystals in a grid or in the direction of each of the elements in order to help your craft. Here are just a few crystals and what they can be used for:

Quartz: substituted for any purpose, cleansing
selenite: can cleanse any crystal from negative energies
Amethyst: can expel negative energies and anxiety
Rose quartz: used to attract love and self love

10. oils can be used in your craft

I find rubbing oils on candle spells really help speed up the process, or even aid in your craft. I enjoy making my own for separate purposes. For example, in my money oil, i use olive oil, patchouli, and basil. You just mix it together and... BAM! you got your own oil for cheap and easy.

11. book of shadows (spell book)

An important tool for witches working on their craft is their book of shadows. A book of shadows is essentially a spell book. It can also be filled with tips and tricks that can help them. A book of shadows can range from a plain spiral notebook to something fancy. As long as it works for you, then its your book of shadows.

12. Use herbs to help your craft

Adding herbs to candle spells or spell pouches can enhance your craft. There are many herbs with different properties to aid your craft. Such as basil, basil is good to work with in prosperity spells. As long as you use the herbs with the intention of your spell, it'll help aid you. Here are just a couple herbs and their metaphysical properties:

Rosemary: can substitute any herb
Bay leaves: can write your intention on them, best used for prosperity.
Mug wort: Banish negativity
patchouli: can be used for prosperity and happiness

13.correctly cleansing your space

Using White sage is a closed practice! Using palo santo is a closed practice! I would only use juniper leaves, cedar, pine, or incense to cleanse my space. I believe using some sage is okay, but I would definitely do some intense research. Cleansing is pretty important, though, to help get rid of negativity. I would at least use some incense.

14.moon water

moon water is an easy tool to use in your craft. It can be used to cleanse negativity from surfaces, or even used as an offering. Its super easy to make moon water too. You take a cup of distilled, boiled, or bottled water, and place it in the moonlight. I would leave it outside overnight, but try to retrieve it as soon as you can in the morning. and boom! you got some moon water.

15. Divination tools

There are several tools you can use to talk to your guides, or whoever else. I would be very careful, though. Make sure to set boundaries where only good entities may talk to you, or even cast a circle of protection before using these tools. You don't want to attract anything bad towards you. Some tools you can use for divination are:

Tarot cards
pendulum
crystal ball
scrying mirror

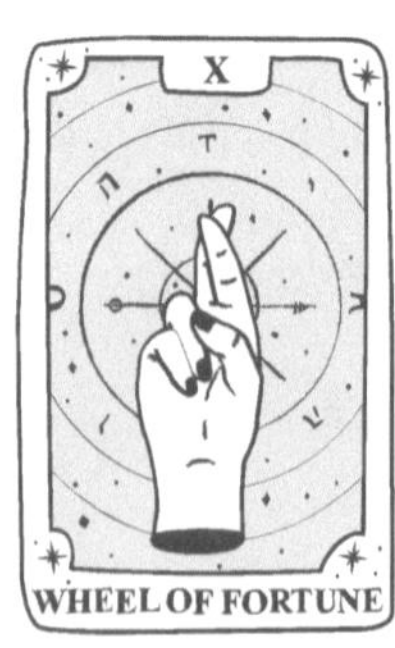

I would definitely do more research before attempting to use any of these divination tools, just to be safe on your end.

16. sigils

marking your candles, journals, or pouches with sigils is another great way to add intention to your craft. The easiest way would to be to use the wheel pictured below. You simply write out an intention, such as " I am wealthy" and follow all the letters in that sentence to draw a sigil from the wheel

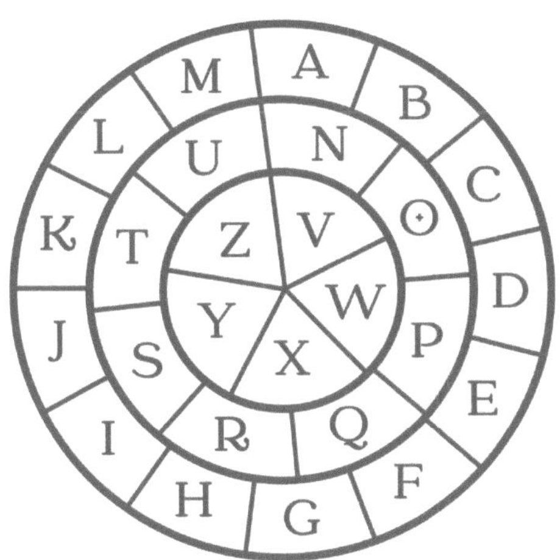

17. learn about chakras

Everyone has chakras throughout their body.
you have the:
Sahasrara- Crown chakra(in charge of thinking)
Ajna- Third eye chakra(psychic vision)
Vishudda- Throat chakra (speaking)
Anahata-Heart chakra (love, healing)
Manipura- solar plexus(personal power)
svadhisthana- sacral chakra (intuition)
Muladhara- Root chakra (grounding)

Each chakra helps control a different part of you,
and its best to meditate and focus on each
different part of the body to fully heal.

18.use solstice energy

Casting spells during any season solstice is great. The world is changing, and you can channel that changing energy to help you change and evolve. You could do something small such as a smoke cleanse or do something big like a spell in the woods. I would do research right before the solstice to see the time the solstice is going into effect.

19. numerology

after you work on your craft and get into it a bit more, you may notice repeating numbers. You'll see numbers like 111 or 222 frequently, and the more you pay attention to them, the more youll see them. these numbers do mean something. pay attention to the sequences, here are some number sequences:

111- means to trust your gut and listen to your heart
222- means youre in the right place in the right time
333- means your guides are sending their love and support
444- the universe and your guides are protecting you
555- something new is coming
666- time to reflect on your spiritual growth
777- Luck, good things are about to happen
888-Balance, everything falling into place
999- let go whats no longer serving you

20.different witch types

You can be whatever witch you wanna be! you can be a Kitchen witch, who uses their powers to cook or bake with intention. You could be a sea witch, who uses the ocean to channel their powers. The possibilities are endless! You could even do your own thing, or a combination of what you'd like. There are plenty of types out there, way too much to list. So do your own research before you choose!

21.Altar space

If you so choose, you may want to have an Altar space to practice your magic. Ther amazing thing about Altars is: they come however you want them to come. You dont even need a dedicated altar space, as long as you have the tools and materials needed for your practice, youll be fine. There are a couple things I like to put on my altar:
incense holder
candles
crystals
offering plate
cedar smudge
a pentacle in the middle for each element

those are just to name a few, but you can make your altar however youd like!

22.bath magic

Another form of magic is bath magic. Its great to bathe in herbs and oils with your baths intentions. Water also helps retain energy you put into it, so if you whisper your intentions into the water, itll help store those energies. One bath spell i always use is a self love spell.
All you need for a self love spell is:
rose petals for self love
lavender for calm
epsom salt for purity
rosemary for self love
lemon balm for calming
red clover for protection
then all you gotta do is mix it up and whisper your intentions! you can also have crystals on the side, i would check and make sure your crystals are water safe.

23. Using the elements to enhance your work

a pretty crucial part of witchcraft is the use of elements. there are 5 elements used in witchcraft. They are:

- Fire: activity, inspiration, passion, courage, risk, impulsiveness, creativity, impatience (Male).
- Water: emotion, love, feeling, empathy, adaptability, secretive, artistic (Female).
- Air: intellect, thinking, communication, ungrounded, flighty, spirited, inventive, questioning (Male).
- Earth: grounded, practical, steady, responsible, work, materialism (Female)
- spirit: basis for law of attraction

there are actually corresponding directions for each of the elements as well.

- Fire - South - Summer - Red/yellow
- Water - West - Autumn - Blue
- Air - East - Spring - Green
- Earth - North - Winter - Brown

the elements are also in the tarot as well.
pentacles-earth
cups-water
swords-air
wants-fire
Pictured below is a pentagram where each othe the elements are positioned. The pentagram is actually used for each of these elements, and is not evil like others believe

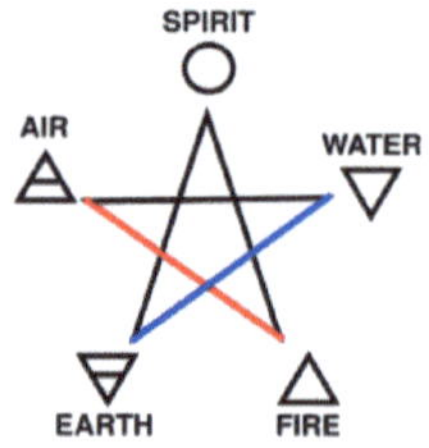

24.listening to your intuition

Your intuition won't be the best when you first start your craft. After you put in the work for yourself,you'll start to notice signs in yourself about what to do or what not to do. Sometimes its in your gut, sometimes its in your heart. Its good to listen to your body, or even your guides if you need clarification. Always sit and meditate on a bigger desicion if need be.

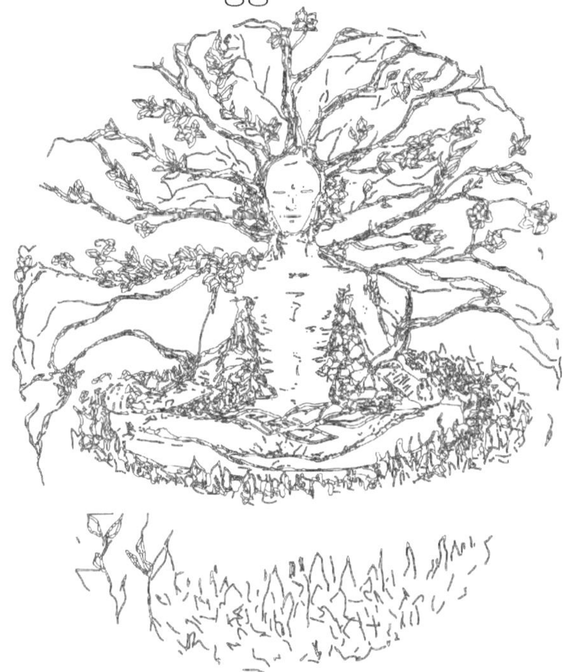

25. Hexing/jinxes

I do not recommend attempting a hex or a jinx as a beginner! The repercussions can be dangerous if done improperly! I also just don't recommend doing them at all. Instead, I would just up your protection, because eventually Karma will come around to those who have harmed you. I strongly recommend working with love and light.

26.meditation

I would say meditation is an important part of your craft. It can Relieve stress, help get your brain back on track, induce calmness, and help connect you to your guides or higer self. I recommend just trying to meditate a couple minutes everyday, maybe even longer if you want to. You'll be able to see the difference in yourself after a couple days.

27.Patience

Patience is Definitely a virtue in witchcraft. you must be patient and wait for spells to come into fruitian, or any manifestations for that matter. Sure, its magic. But it wakes time, as do all things. Some spells and manifestations come quicker than others, so please, wait and see what the universe has in store for you.

28.Karma

You may or may not believe in karma, its certainly up to you. Karma is based upon the energy you or anyone else puts out into the universe. If someone is mean to you or has done you horribly wrong, the universe will come around and bite them back eventually, as is the karmic cycle. There is no time limit on a karmic cycle, it just happens when it happens. That's also another reason why you need to be patient, lol. Bottom line is, be kind to others and put good energy out into the universe, and you'll receive good back.

Easy Beginner spells

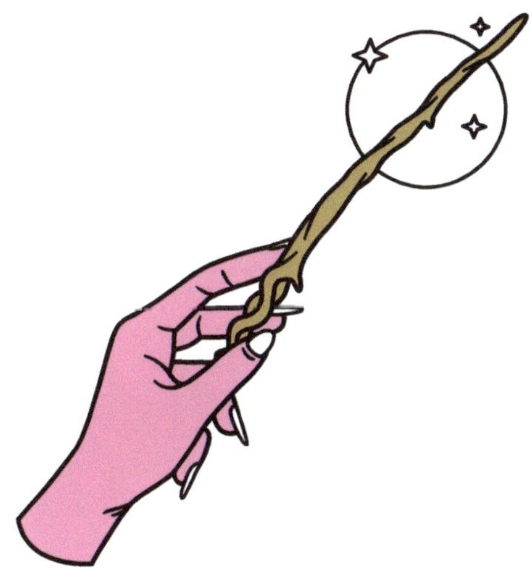

money spells

Money Bowl

get a bowl of your choice and cleanse with moon water,
insence, or smudge of your choice
Then fill the bowl with:
Rice- for abundance
basil- for cash
rosemary- for abundance
bay leaves- write your intention on them
green adventurine, pyrite, or jade
cinnamon- for abundance
add coins and money
you then want to put a green candle in and light it. keep
filling the bowl with spare change until you get the
money you desire. Then give that change to someone in
need.

<u>Candle spell</u>

grab a green candle, and carve a money sigil of
your choice in there
coat the candle in an oil of your choice, then roll
it through:
alfalfa- abundance
patchouli- prosperity
basil-abundance
rosemary- prosperity
and red clover for protection
you will then night the candle, and do a chant of
your choice if you so choose. There are plenty to
choose from. One of my favorites is:
Money comes to me easily.
money comes to me fast.
abundance doesn't miss me.
financial stability will last

love spells

I don't recommend using a love spell if the person is not into you, as it can have negative effects. I do however have ways you can sweeten a bond with someone if you so choose.

Apple spell
take an apple and cut it in half. Then take a picture of you, and then a picture of your partner and place it on opposite sides.
then you put on each of you:
honey to sweeten things up
sugar to sweeten things up.
red clover for protection
rose petals for love
and catnip for happiness
youll then close the apple, and wrap it in twine. keep that apple on yout altar till you notice that things are sweetening up. then you should bury it.

<u>Self love spell</u>

for this spell, you'll take a jar and cleanse it.
Then, youll fill the jar with:
Himalayan salt for protection
honey so you can be sweet
sugar for sweetness
lavender for calm
rose petals for self love
rosemary for self love
and rose quartz for self love

youll then close the car and seal it with a pink
candle. and boom! you got a self love jar.

ᴆream spell

one way I like to ensure I have sweet
dreams is a dream pouch
you'll need to cleanse a pouch, then fill
it with:
lavender for calmness
catnip for happiness
blue kyanite for good dreams
and rose petals for sweet dreams
all you do is close the bag, and put it in
your pillow for sweet dreams

luck spell

<u>Luck charm</u>

you could always enchant an item you carry around you to be lucky. Hold your item close to your chest, meditate on it, and say
"I enchant this item to aid in making me lucky. so mote it be."
or something to that effect. use your own words to enchant what feels right

Epilogue

witchcraft is what you make of it. I hope using these tips and trick will help you on your journey. It's always a great idea to do your own research and do things at your own pace. Do and feel what's right to you. Your craft is about YOU. Please remember that. I'm glad you're here, and that we're able to explore the path of witchcraft together. Blessed be <3